WORLD OF INSECTS

Cockroaches

by Emily K. Green

BELLWETHER MEDIA · MINNEAPOLIS, MN

BLASTOFF!
2
READERS

Note to Librarians, Teachers, and Parents:

Blastoff! Readers are carefully developed by literacy experts and combine standards-based content with developmentally appropriate text.

Level 1 provides the most support through repetition of high-frequency words, light text, predictable sentence patterns, and strong visual support.

Level 2 offers early readers a bit more challenge through varied simple sentences, increased text load, and less repetition of high-frequency words.

Level 3 advances early-fluent readers toward fluency through increased text and concept load, less reliance on visuals, longer sentences, and more literary language.

Whichever book is right for your reader, Blastoff! Readers are the perfect books to build confidence and encourage a love of reading that will last a lifetime!

This edition first published in 2007 by Bellwether Media.

No part of this publication may be reproduced in whole or in part without written permission of the publisher. For information regarding permission, write to Bellwether Media Inc., Attention: Permissions Department, Post Office Box 1C, Minnetonka, MN 55345-9998.

Library of Congress Cataloging-in-Publication Data
Green, Emily K., 1966–
  Cockroaches / by Emily K. Green.
    p. cm. — (Blastoff! readers) (World of insects)
Summary: "Simple text accompanied by full-color photographs give an up-close look at cockroaches."
  Includes bibliographical references and index.
  ISBN-10: 1-60014-010-6 (hardcover : alk. paper)
  ISBN-13: 978-1-60014-010-5 (hardcover : alk. paper)
  1. Cockroaches—Juvenile literature. I. Title. II. Series.

QL505.5.G735 2006
595.7'28—dc22   2006001995

Text copyright © 2007 by Bellwether Media.
Printed in the United States of America.

Table of Contents

Cockroaches are **insects**.

Most cockroaches are
black or brown.

Their bodies are shaped like **ovals**.

Hard shells cover their bodies.

All cockroaches have six
legs. They run fast.

Most cockroaches have wings but they do not fly.

antennas

Cockroaches have **antennas**.
Cockroaches use antennas to
look for food.

cerci

Cockroaches have **cerci**.
Cockroaches use cerci to
sense danger.

11

Shiny **wax** coats the body
of a cockroach.

Cockroaches have flat
bodies. They can squeeze
through tiny cracks.

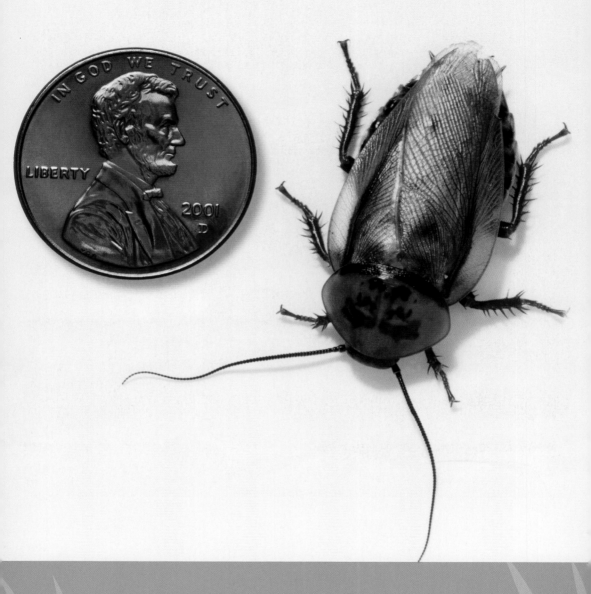

Some cockroaches are small.

Some cockroaches are big.
One kind of cockroach is as
big as a mouse.

Cockroaches live everywhere but the coldest places on Earth.

Most cockroaches live in **tropical rainforests** where it is warm and wet.

Some cockroaches live in houses and other buildings.

Cockroaches hide in dark places during the day. They come out at night to eat.

Cockroaches can eat your food! They also eat paper, plants, or dead animals.

But when the lights come on
cockroaches scurry away.

Glossary

antennas—the long, thin feelers on an insect's head; cockroaches use the feelers to touch and smell things.

cerci—the short, pointy feelers at the back of the cockroach's body; cockroaches use the cerci to sense how the air moves.

insect—a kind of animal that has a hard body; most insects also have two antennas, six legs, and two or four wings.

oval—an egg shape

tropical rainforests—forests that grow in the warmest, wettest parts of Earth

wax—a smooth, slippery material found in nature

To Learn More

AT THE LIBRARY

Cannon, Janell. *Crickwing.* San Diego: Harcourt, 2000.

Greenaway, Theresa. *Big Book of Bugs.* New York: Dorling Kindersley, 2000.

Horowitz, Ruth. *Breakout at the Bug Lab.* New York: Dial Books, 2001.

Moreton, Daniel. *La Cucaracha Martina: A Caribbean Folktale.* New York: Turtle Books, 1997.

O'Malley, Kevin. *Leo Cockroach: Toy Tester.* New York: Walker and Co., 1999.

ON THE WEB
Learning more about cockroaches is as easy as 1, 2, 3.

WWW.FACTSURFER.COM

1. Go to www.factsurfer.com

2. Enter "cockroaches" into search box.

3. Click the "Surf" button and you will see a list of related web sites.

With factsurfer.com, finding more information is just a click away.

Index

The photographs in this book are reproduced through the courtesy of: Holt Studios International Ltd.,/Alamy, front cover; davies & starr/Getty Images, p. 4; Dwight Kuhn Photography, pp. 5, 20; GK and Vikki Hart/Getty Images, pp. 6, 14; Andre Maritz, p. 7; Paul Topp, p. 8; Karen Beard/ Getty Images, p. 9; Frank Greenaway/Getty Images, p. 10; Carles Nesbit/Getty Images, pp. 11; Mark Hayes, p. 12; David Coder/Getty Images, p. 13; Arlene Jean Gee, p. 14(inset); AFP/Getty Images, p. 15; JH Pete/Getty Images, pp. 16-17; Vadim Kozlovsky, p. 18; David Maitland/Getty Images, p. 19; James H. MacAllister, p. 21.